monday morning

HANDS-ON PRIMARY PROJECTS

By Dana McMillan of the Learning Exchange, Inc.
of Kansas City, Missouri
Illustrated by Corbin Hillam

Publisher: Roberta Suid
Contributing Editors: Elizabeth Russell,
Lillian Lieberman
Cover Design: David Hale
Design and Production: Mary Francis
Contributing Artist: Donna Swafford-Cushman

ISBN 0-912107-20-0

Printed in the United States of America

9 8 7 6 5 4 3 2 1

CONTENTS

Neanderthal Ned and the Dinosaur   83

Vanishing Act *(sequencing size)*
Big Bones *(measuring length)*
Scrambled Dinosaur Eggs *(recognizing words)*
Neanderthal Ned's Board Game *(reinforcing skills)*
Neanderthal Ned Bulletin Board
Dinosaur Art

Dana's Department Store   97

How to Make Dana's Department Store
Store Sorting Cards *(categorizing)*
Money Cards *(recognizing coin values)*
Store Bulletin Board

INTRODUCTION

This activity book uses a thematic approach to classroom management. Designed by and for early childhood teachers, all of the activities in the book have been tested by teachers of preschool — third grade students.

Teaching all curriculum objectives through a single theme is an effective method of organizing early childhood lesson plans. The young children we work with have been delighted with the seven themes in this book: Farmers Fred and Frieda, the Gingerbread Man, Super Shape Hero, Wake Up! It's Spring, Safety Kid, Neanderthal Ned and the Dinosaur, and Dana's Department Store. Each chapter contains:

- A pattern for each character which may be used on all activities. These patterns may also be used on letters to parents, awards, and flannel board activities.

- Directions for making activities designed to teach reading readiness, math, and writing skills.

- Specific patterns for each activity.

- Game boards for practice in a variety of skills.

- Directions for making bulletin board characters which introduce the theme and also teach skills.

We encourage you to look at the style of each activity as well as its objective. Don't avoid a theme because it has an activity that teaches color words, for example, when your students are not ready for color words. You can easily substitute number recognition for color words in the same activity and theme.

We developed the activities in this book to solve classroom challenges common to all teachers.

- Storage - Most of the activities, including the game boards, use file folders. The activity can be labeled with the name of the skill and stored in a file drawer or box when not in use.

- Flexibility - Activities can be laminated or covered with clear contact paper, on which students can write with a transparency pen. In this way, the same activity can be used to teach beginning sounds with a group of five-year-olds and shape recognition with three-year-olds.

• Teacher's time - Since preparation time is limited, we have provided patterns for all activities. In most cases you only need to duplicate, color, cut out, and glue on patterns.

• Curriculum objectives - You will find the activities deal with very specific objectives. Often these activities do not rely on reading ability. We have included the skills most commonly taught in early childhood classes, with special emphasis on sequencing ability. We have been delighted with the appeal of these materials. It is wonderful to hear teachers who came reluctantly to a workshop express great excitement when they found they could easily produce a new set of activities to take back to their classrooms. We hope this book will make it possible for you to experience that same excitement.

These activities were developed by The Learning Exchange, a non-profit educational resource center which helps school districts improve quality of instruction. For more information contact:
Resource Center Coordinator
The Learning Exchange, Inc.
2720 Walnut
Kansas City, Missouri 64108
(816) 471-0455

Chapter One: Farmer Fred and Frieda

Fred and Frieda's Apple Business

Picture cards tell the story of apples from tree to pie.

SKILL: Sequencing story cards

MATERIALS:
Colored file folder
Five cards cut from card stock 4" x 4 1/2"
Zip lock bag

CONSTRUCTION:
1. Color, cut out, and glue the title and apple on the front of the file folder.
2. Color, cut out, and glue sequence cards on card stock.
3. Staple a zip lock bag inside the file folder to store the sequence cards.
4. Print these directions inside the cover of the file folder: Put these cards in order to tell a story.

PROCEDURE:
1. This activity is for one student working alone.
2. Have the student sequence the cards. You may wish to ask the student to tell a story to go along with the cards.

EXTENSIONS:
● Ask students to tell their own versions of Fred and Frieda's apple business. They may wish to draw their own pictures to make sequence cards.
● Hold up two cards and ask, "Which came first? second?" etc. Encourage students to answer with the words first, second, third, fourth, or fifth.

Fred and Frieda's Apple Business

Sequencing
Cards

APPLES- 5¢
APPLE
CIDER- 50¢
APPLE
BUTTER- 75¢

FRIEDA'S
APPLE
STAND

Hands-on Primary Projects © 1984 Monday Morning Books

Fred and Frieda's Farm Animals

Students match pictures of mother and baby animals.

SKILL: Matching

MATERIALS:
File folder
16 cards cut from card stock 3" x 3 1/2"
Zip lock bag

CONSTRUCTION:
1. Color, cut out, and glue patterns of Fred and Frieda on the front of the file folder.
2. Print on front of folder: "Farmers Fred and Frieda are worried. All of the babies on the farm are mixed up. Help put the babies back with their mothers."
3. Color, cut out, and glue the pictures to the cards.
4. Staple a zip lock bag inside folder to store cards.

PROCEDURE:
1. This activity may be used with one or two students.
2. Challenge students to match pictures of mother animals with correct babies.

EXTENSION:
• Use these cards to play a concentration-style memory game with two to five players. Turn all the cards face down. One student turns over two cards. If they match, the student keeps them. If not, the student turns them over again and gives someone else a turn. Winner has the most pairs.

Fred and Frieda's Farm Animals

Hands-on Primary Projects © 1984 Monday Morning Books

Fred and Frieda's Farm Animals

Fred and Frieda's Farm Animals

Apron Patterns

Students match fabric patterns in a memory game.

SKILL: Matching

MATERIALS:
Large manila envelope
12 cards cut from card stock 4" x 7"
Tiny print wallpaper (from sample books)

CONSTRUCTION:
1. Cut out the large apron and glue it on the front of the manila envelope.
2. Color and cut out 12 copies of Frieda. Glue one on each card.
3. Use the small apron pattern to cut out pairs of aprons from the wallpaper. Glue aprons on Frieda to make six pairs.

PROCEDURE:
1. This is a game for one to four players.
2. You may wish to demonstrate the way to play as described on the envelope to help students learn the rules.

EXTENSIONS:
● Make more than six pairs of aprons or keep adding new pairs as students progress in recognizing patterns.
● Prepare the game with pairs of solid color aprons to create a color recognition activity.

APRON PATTERNS
PLAYERS 1-4
Directions:

Lay the cards in rows face down. Turn over two cards. If the aprons match, keep the cards and take another turn. If they don't match, turn them face down again. The next player takes a turn. Continue until all the aprons are matched. The player with the most pairs wins.

Hands-on Primary Projects © 1984 Monday Morning Books

Apron Patterns

Hands-on Primary Projects © 1984 Monday Morning Books

Egg-citing

Students learn the stages of development of a chick.

SKILL: Sequencing

MATERIALS:
Colored file folder
Five cards cut from card stock 4" x 4"
Oaktag circle cut to fit the sequence wheel
Small paper brad
Zip lock bag

CONSTRUCTION:
1. Color the sequence wheel with flesh tones for early stages and yellow for later stages.
2. Cut out and glue the sequence wheel to the oaktag circle.
3. Cut out oval title and glue it to front of file folder.
4. Use an exacto knife to cut out the wedge-shaped viewer.
5. Attach the sequence wheel inside the cover of the file folder with the paper brad. Line up the wheel with the opening so that one stage of the chick shows at a time.
6. Color and cut out sequence cards.
7. Glue each card to a piece of card stock.
8. Staple zip lock bag inside file folder to store cards.

PROCEDURE:
1. This is an activity for one student.
2. Have student turn the sequence wheel to see the stages of chick development in the egg.
3. Challenge student to arrange the sequence cards to show the chick hatching.

Cut out. Then use as pattern to cut wedge in file folder.

Egg-citing _____

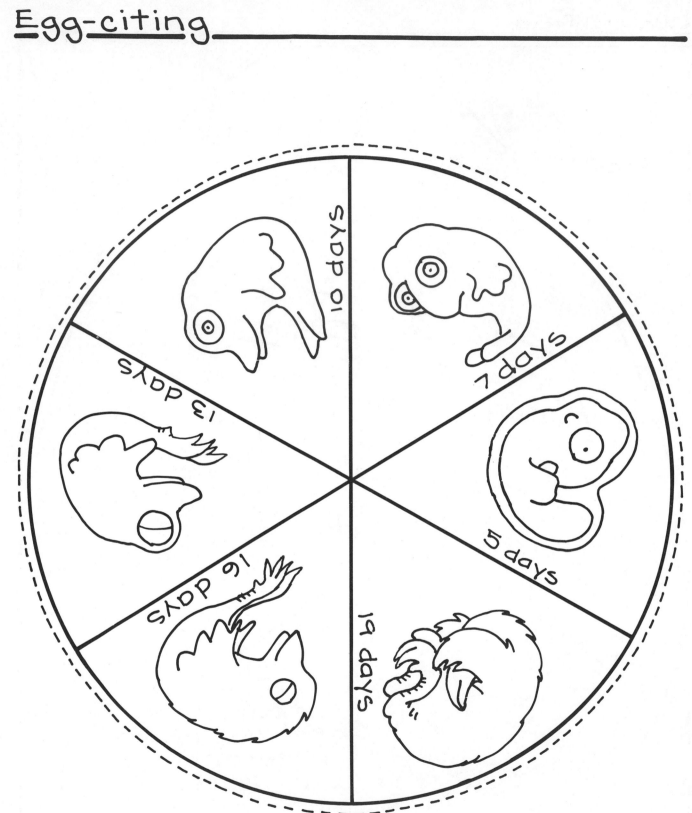

Hands-on Primary Projects © 1984 Monday Morning Books

Egg-citing

Sequencing
Cards

Bird's-Eye View of the Farm

This game board can reinforce a variety of skills.

SKILL: To be chosen by teacher

MATERIALS:
Green poster board
White 3/4" peel-off dots
Construction paper (brown, yellow, green, blue)

CONSTRUCTION:
1. Trace the patterns and cut out the trees, barn, silo, tractor, garden, and pond from construction paper.
2. Glue the shapes onto the posterboard.
3. Form the game track with peel-off dots.
4. Laminate or cover with clear contact paper.
5. Write skills on the game track with an erasable transparency pen so that you can change the skills as the students progress.

PROCEDURE:
1. Two to four students may play this game.
2. First player rolls a die and moves that number of spaces. To stay there, player must answer skills problem correctly. If incorrect, player returns to original space.
3. Play continues until someone lands directly on Finish.

Bird's-Eye View of the Farm

Pockets Bulletin Board

Students sort pictures of things according to vowel sounds.

SKILL: Recognizing long and short vowel sounds

MATERIALS:
Two sheets of oaktag 22" x 24"
Wallpaper in various patterns
Seven library pockets
3" x 5" index cards
Pictures of words with long and short vowel sounds

CONSTRUCTION:
1. Enlarge the pattern of Fred and Frieda with an opaque or over-head projector and trace onto oaktag. Make the figures about two feet tall, a good size for bulletin board use.
2. Use wallpaper to make the clothes and Fred's hat.
3. Glue two library pockets on Fred's overalls and five library pockets on Frieda's apron.
4. Cut out pictures from old workbooks or magazines and glue on index cards.
5. Print "Long Vowels" and "Short Vowels" on Fred's pockets.
6. Print "a," "e," "i," "o," and "u" on Frieda's pockets.

PROCEDURE:
1. This activity is for one or two students.
2. Hang this activity on a low bulletin board so that students can stand as they sort cards into the proper pockets.

Chapter Two: The Gingerbread Man

Sequence the Story

Students put pictures in order to retell a familiar story.

SKILL: Chronological sequencing

MATERIALS:
File folder
Seven cards cut from card stock 6" x 5"
Brown and pink construction paper
Zip lock bag

CONSTRUCTION:
1. Trace the smaller Gingerbread Man pattern onto brown paper and the larger one onto pink paper. Cut out and glue together.
2. Draw on eyes, nose, mouth, tie, and buttons with a fine felt-tip pen.
3. Glue the Gingerbread Man on the front of the file folder and print: "The Gingerbread Man — Put his story in order, but watch out for the fox!"
4. Color the story pictures. Cut out and glue onto cards.
5. Staple zip lock bag inside folder to store cards.

PROCEDURE:
1. Have the student put the story cards in any order which makes sense to him or her.
2. Ask the student to tell you the story.

EXTENSION:
● Glue a strip of felt to the back of each laminated story card. Use the story cards on a flannel board as a visual while telling the story.

Sequence the Story

Sequence the Story

Hands-on Primary Projects © 1984 Monday Morning Books

Cookie Count

Students match dots to numerals.

SKILL: Associating numerals and quantities

MATERIALS:
Oaktag cut 18" x 24"
Pink and brown construction paper
Small coin envelope or zip lock bag

CONSTRUCTION:
1. Trace the patterns. Cut 10 big gingerbread men and 10 circles from pink paper, 10 small men from brown.
2. Print numerals 1–10 on pink circles. Glue a circle to each brown gingerbread man. Draw features on each shape, then glue to pink gingerbread men. Glue all 10 to chart.
3. Trace the patterns and cut out 10 larger cookie shapes from brown paper, 10 smaller cookie shapes from pink paper.
4. Make chocolate chips in the cookies with a hole punch. In each pink cookie, punch a number of holes to correspond to a numeral on the chart. Glue pink cookies to brown ones.
5. Store cookies in coin envelope or zip lock bag.

PROCEDURE:
1. This is an activity for one student.
2. Have the student match the number of chocolate chips in a cookie with the correct numeral on a gingerbread man.

EXTENSION:
● Laminate chart and cookies. Put a generous amount of rubber cement on the back of each cookie, allow to air dry. The cookies will stick to the chart for weeks. When they lose their stickiness, add more rubber cement.

Cookie Count

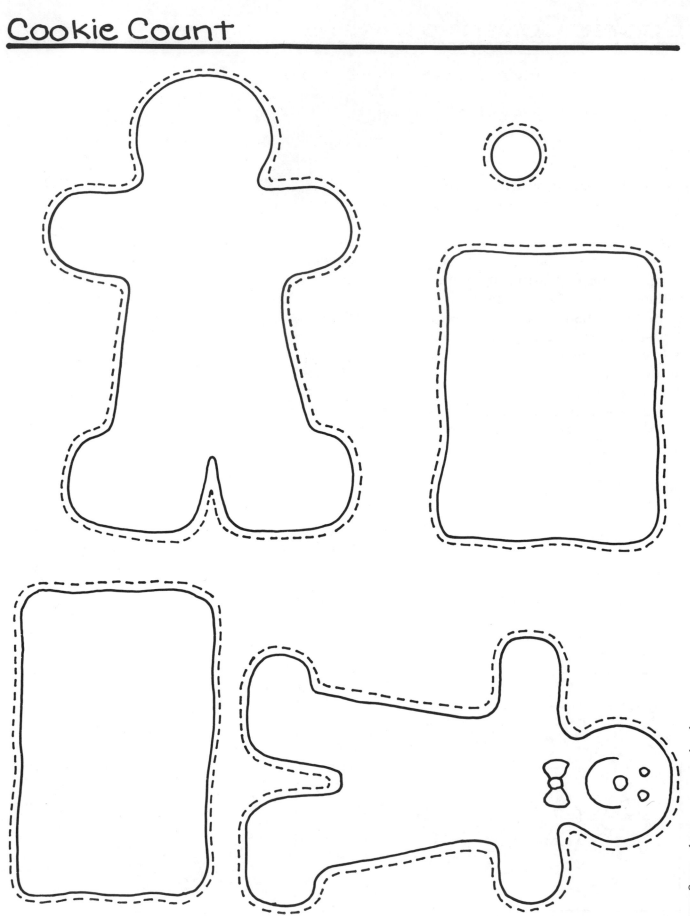

Hands-on Primary Projects © 1984 Monday Morning Books

Paper Bag Puppets

Students tell the story with their own words and gestures.

SKILL: Dramatic play

MATERIALS:
Seven brown paper lunch bags
Colored construction paper
Glue or paste

CONSTRUCTION:
1. Trace the puppet patterns onto appropriate colors of construction paper. (Example: manila for the old woman's face and white for her hair.) Cut out all pieces.
2. Glue the pieces of face and head to bottom of bag.
3. Glue mouth to side of bag directly in line with head.

PROCEDURE:
1. Several students can perform this activity.
2. Create a puppet stage in a doorway or above a table.
3. Have students use the puppets to act out the story.

Paper Bag Puppets

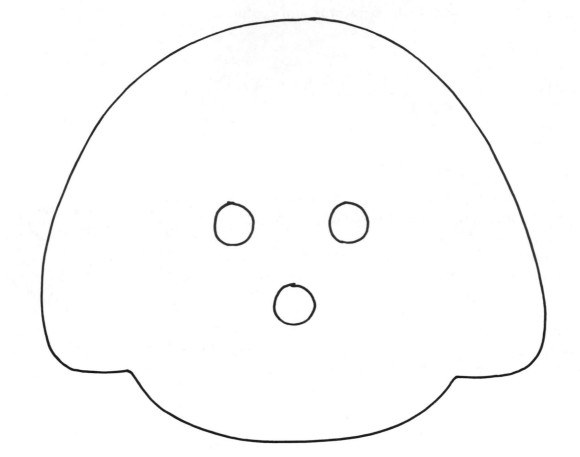

GINGERBREAD
MAN

Hands-on Primary Projects © 1984 Monday Morning Books

Paper Bag Puppets

Paper Bag Puppets

COW

Hands-on Primary Projects © 1984 Monday Morning Books

Paper Bag Puppets

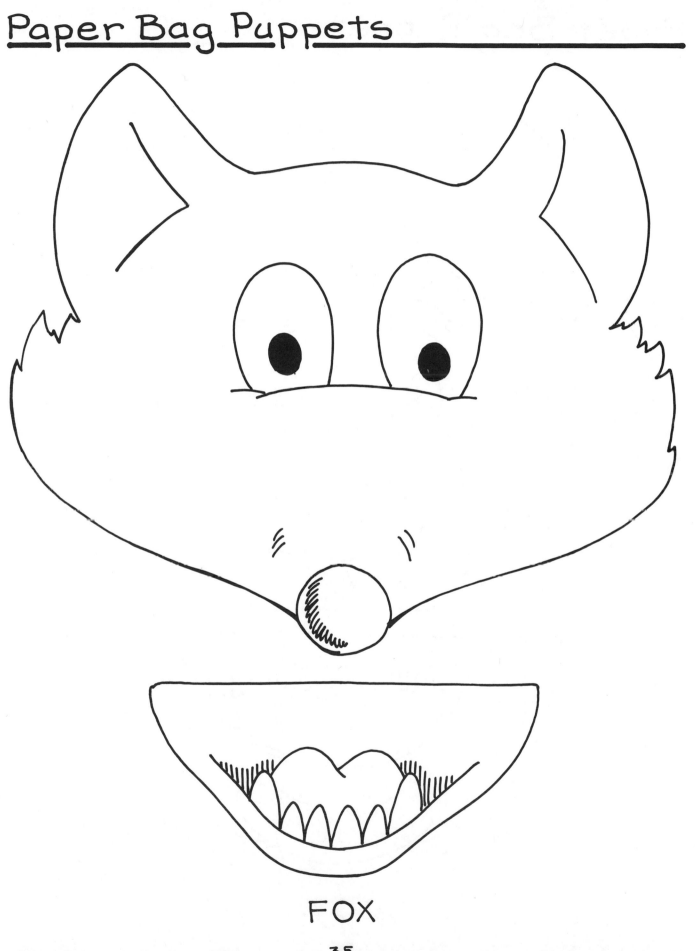

FOX

Paper Bag Puppets

BOY

Hands-on Primary Projects © 1984 Monday Morning Books

Paper Bag Puppets

OLD LADY

Paper Bag Puppets

OLD MAN

Hands-on Primary Projects © 1984 Monday Morning Books

Paper Bag Puppets

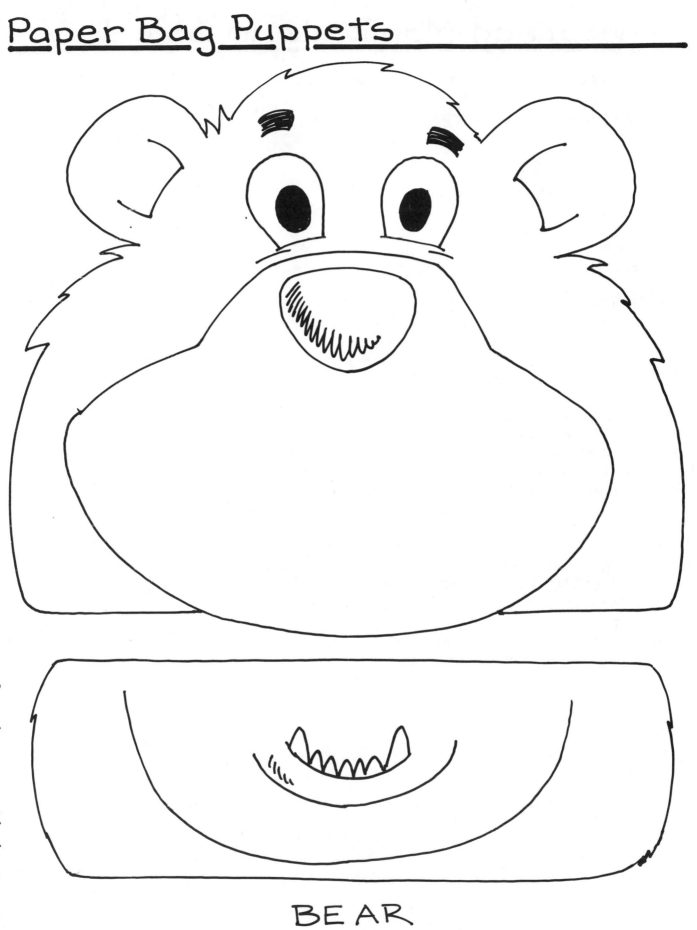

BEAR

Gingerbread Man Bulletin Board

Students read body parts words on a large paper figure.

SKILL: Identifying body parts and their words

MATERIALS:
Pink and brown poster board
Small piece of pink floral wrapping paper
Four 2" buttons
Six or seven smaller buttons
Sentence strips
Heavy paper for arrows

CONSTRUCTION:
1. Enlarge the Gingerbread Man on page 25 with an opaque projector or a transparency and an overhead projector.
2. Cut out the large figure from pink poster board, the small one from brown poster board. Glue them together.
3. Cut the bow out of wrapping paper and glue it on.
4. Glue on large buttons for eyes and shirt buttons, small buttons for mouth. (Use white glue. Add buttons after laminating.) Draw nose with felt-tip pen.
5. Write each of these words on a sentence strip: head, arms, body, legs, eyes, nose, mouth.
6. Cut arrows out of heavy paper.

PROCEDURE:
1. Hang Gingerbread Man on a bulletin board. Add letters which say: NOW PRESENTING — THE GINGERBREAD MAN.
2. Display the word strips around the Gingerbread Man. Pin arrows to bulletin board to connect words and body parts.
3. Have students remove all of the arrows, mix up the words, and test each other by replacing the arrows correctly.

Gingerbread Man Game

Students add or subtract to reach the Finish.

SKILLS: Addition and subtraction

MATERIALS:
Oaktag 12" x 18"
Peel-off dots in two colors

CONSTRUCTION:
1. Color, cut out, and glue the patterns on the oaktag.
2. Connect the pictures with a game track of peel-off dots. Use one color for the plus and minus signs, the other for the spaces between.

PROCEDURE:
1. Two to four students may play this game.
2. Each student rolls a die and moves that number of spaces. If the student lands on a plus or minus sign, he or she must roll the die and make an additional move, either forward (+) or back (-) the indicated number of spaces.
3. Play continues until the first child arrives at Finish.

Gingerbread Man Game

Hands-on Primary Projects © 1984 Monday Morning Books

Chapter Three: Super Shape Hero

Shape Card Game

One deck of cards serves two games for shape recognition.

SKILL: Identifying shapes

MATERIALS:
30 cards cut from heavy card stock 3 1/2" x 5"
Zip lock bag

CONSTRUCTION:
1. Draw one shape on each card. Make six cards of each shape (oval, square, rectangle, circle, triangle). Be sure shapes do not show on backs of cards.
2. Store cards in zip lock bag.

PROCEDURE:
1. Shape Matching Card Game
   a. Three students may play.
   b. Shuffle the deck and place it face down.
   c. Each student turns up a card and names the shape. Players do this again, trying to match the first shape. If cards match, student keeps the pair. If they do not match, student must put one into a discard pile. After second round, players may pick from deck or discard pile.
   d. Winner has the most pairs when all cards are played.
2. Shape Memory Game
   a. One to five students may play this game.
   b. Shuffle cards and arrange face down in rows.
   c. Play according to rules for Concentration.

Super Shape Sort

Students sort cards in three different ways.

SKILL: Categorizing by size, color, and shape

MATERIALS:
Large clasp envelope
20 cards cut from card stock 5" x 5"

CONSTRUCTION:
1. Color each shape with a different crayon. Color the shape only, not the body parts.
2. Cut out and glue each shape onto a 5" x 5" card.
3. Color, cut out, and glue the picture of the Shape Hero to the front of the clasp envelope. Print:
    SUPER SHAPE SORT
    HELP SUPER SHAPE HERO SORT THE CARDS
    BY COLOR, SIZE, AND SHAPE

PROCEDURE:
1. Gather students together and demonstrate the use of the Super Shape Sort cards. First show sorting by color. Next demonstrate sorting by size, then by shape.
2. After the demonstration, make individual assignments. Some students may only sort by color, while others may be able to do two steps or all three.

Super Shape Sort

Hands-on Primary Projects © 1984 Monday Morning Books

Super Shape Sort

Super Shape Sort

Super Shape Sort

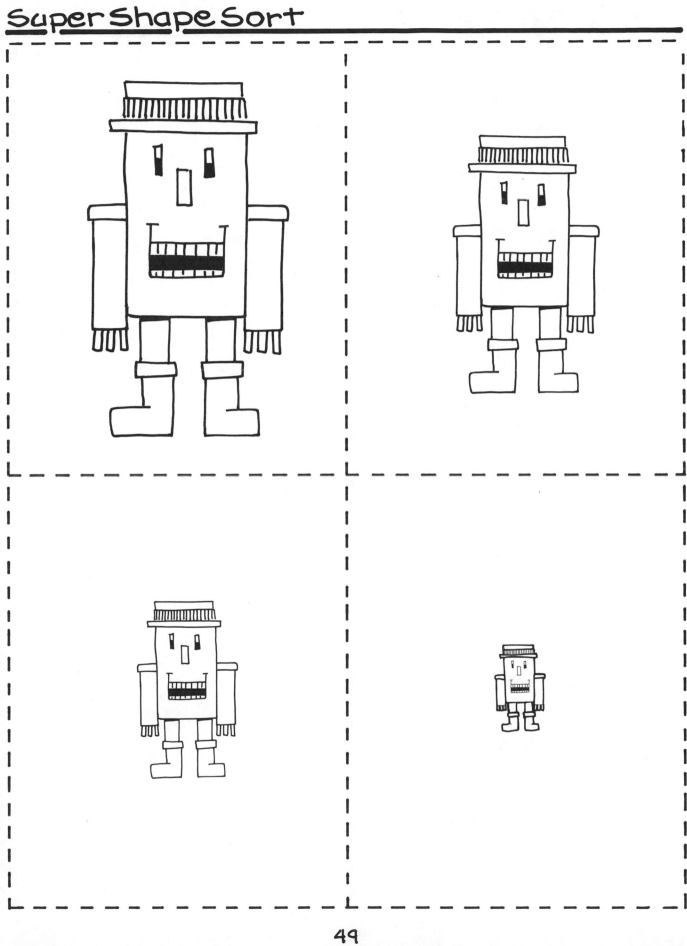

Super Shape Sort

Shape Art

Students use paper shapes to follow patterns and make them.

SKILL: Creating pictures with shapes

MATERIALS:
Pocket folder
Construction paper

CONSTRUCTION:
1. Color the Super Shape Hero and the title. Cut out the figure, title, and the direction bubble and glue them to the front of the pocket folder.
2. Laminate worksheets and construction paper.
3. Cut shapes from construction paper.
4. Store shapes in one pocket, worksheets in the other.

PROCEDURE:
1. Have students place construction paper shapes over the outlines of shapes on the worksheets.
2. Encourage students to arrange the shapes to create their own pictures.

EXTENSION:
● Provide unlaminated colored paper shapes, large pieces of paper, and glue for students to make original shape pictures. Students may hang these up for display or take them home.

Shape Art

Directions:

① Use the shapes in the pocket to match the shapes on the worksheet.

② Use the shapes to make your own pictures.

SHAPE ART

Hands-on Primary Projects © 1984 Monday Morning Books

Shape Art

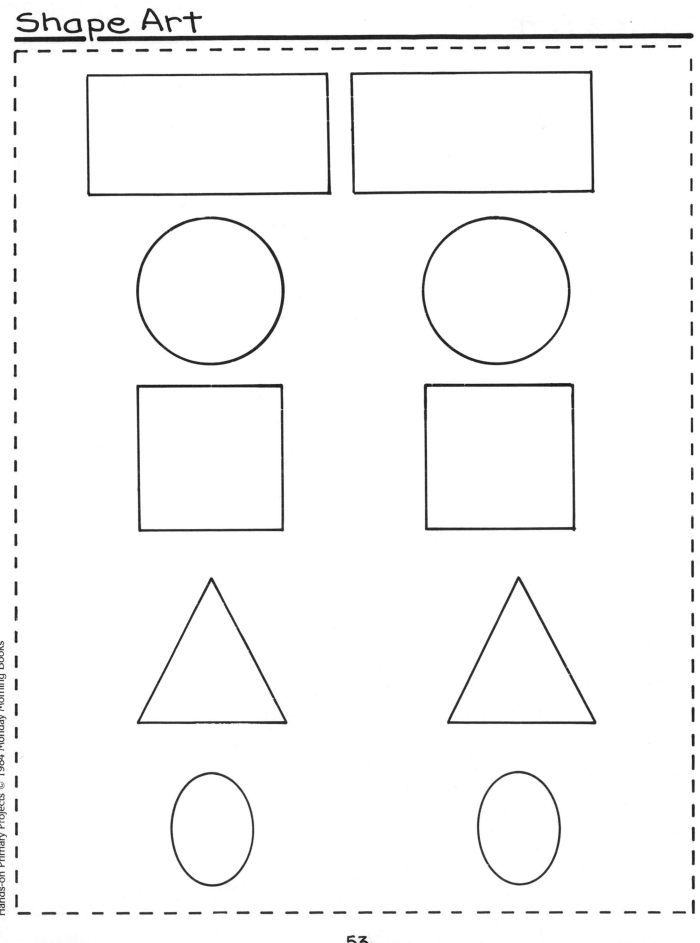

Shape Art

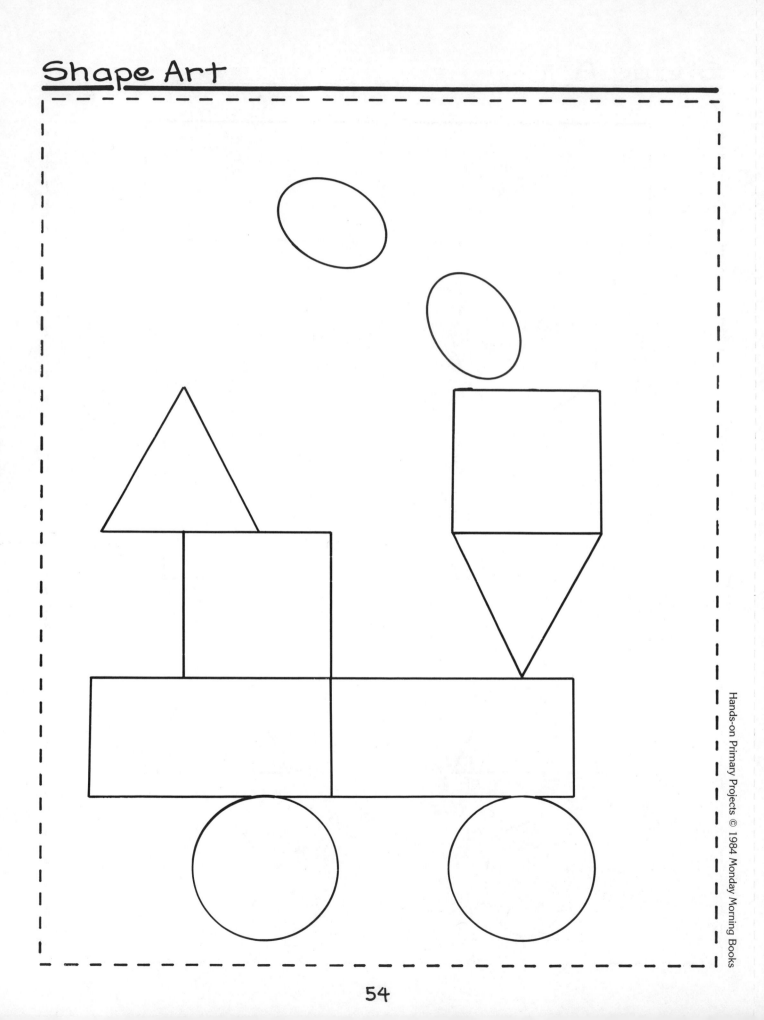

Hands-on Primary Projects © 1984 Monday Morning Books

Super Shape Hero Game Board

Students must identify shapes to move along gameboard.

SKILL: Recognizing shapes

MATERIALS:
Poster board cut 12" x 18"
15 cards cut 3 1/2" x 5"
Zip lock bag

CONSTRUCTION:
1. Color Super Shape Hero on the game track and glue it to the poster board. Do not color shapes on game track.
2. Color, cut out, and glue shape figures to gameboard.
3. Draw a shape on each card. Use each shape three times, for a total of 15 cards.
4. Store cards in zip lock bag.

PROCEDURE:
1. Two to four students may play. Use a die or spinner to determine order of play.
2. Each player in turn draws a card and names the shape on it. That player then moves to the nearest corresponding shape on the gameboard. After each turn the card is placed on the bottom of the deck.
3. Play continues until one player reaches Finish.

EXTENSION:
● For students who are reading, print shape words on cards instead of drawing pictures. Students must read shape word in order to move to that shape on the gameboard.

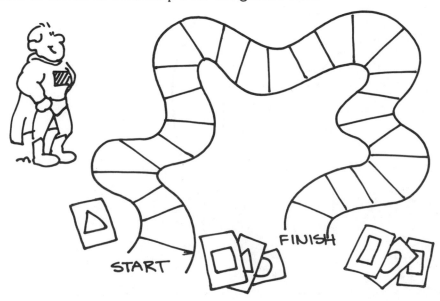

Super Shape Hero Game Board

START

Super Shape Hero Game Board

FINISH

Draw a shape card. Move to the first shape like it on the game board. First player to FINISH wins.

Hands-on Primary Projects © 1984 Monday Morning Books

Super Shape Hero Bulletin Board

This large display introduces characters in this chapter.

SKILL: Recognizing shapes

MATERIALS:
Oaktag
Construction paper

CONSTRUCTION:
1. Enlarge the patterns of Super Shape Hero on page 43 and the shape people on pages 46 – 50 with an opaque projector or a transparency and an overhead projector.
2. Color and cut out the figures.
3. Cut out construct

SUPER SHAPE HERO	MRS. OVAL	MR. SQUARE
MR. RECTANGLE	MISS CIRCLE	TINY TRIANGLE

4. Staple the figures and their names on a bulletin board. If possible, display this chapter's activities nearby.

Chapter Four: Wake Up! It's Spring.

Check-It Chicken

Students name a missing digit, then find answer inside egg.

SKILL: Completing a number sequence

MATERIALS:
Heavy white paper
Small paper brads
Clasp envelope or zip lock bag

CONSTRUCTION:
1. Trace the patterns on heavy white paper. Cut out and cut apart egg halves. Each Check-It Chicken has three parts.
2. Color chicks yellow, background green.
3. For each Check-It Chicken, write a three-number sequence as follows: the first and third numbers on the egg shells, the second number on the chick. Examples: 6-8, 3-5, 2-4. For older students: 276-278, 319-321, 780-782.
4. Use a paper brad to assemble the three pieces.
5. Store the chickens in an envelope or zip lock bag.

PROCEDURE:
1. The student takes an egg and tells the missing number.
2. The student checks the answer by opening the egg and looking at the number on the chick.

EXTENSION:
● Make this activity for sequences such as days of the week, months of the year, and alphabetical order.

Check-It Chicken

The Flower Pot

Partners check each other's knowledge of beginning sounds.

SKILL: Recognizing sounds

MATERIALS:
Construction paper (pink, yellow, purple, orange)
Tongue depressors
White glue
Small pictures of objects which exemplify beginning sounds
Styrofoam
Flower pot

CONSTRUCTION:
1. Trace and cut pink, purple, and orange flowers.
2. Trace and cut yellow faces and glue to flowers.
3. Punch a hole on each petal and glue a small picture beside it.
4. Print the correct answer on the back of each petal.
5. Glue a tongue depressor securely on each flower.
6. Plant flowers in flower pot filled with styrofoam.

PROCEDURE:
1. Pair up students, giving one a flower and one a pencil.
2. One child puts the pencil in a flower hole and tells the letter with which that picture begins.
3. The other child responds to each answer with "correct" or "try again." Students alternate tasks.

EXTENSION:
• Make flowers for skills such as ending sounds, vowel sounds, addition and subtraction, color recognition.

The Flower Pot

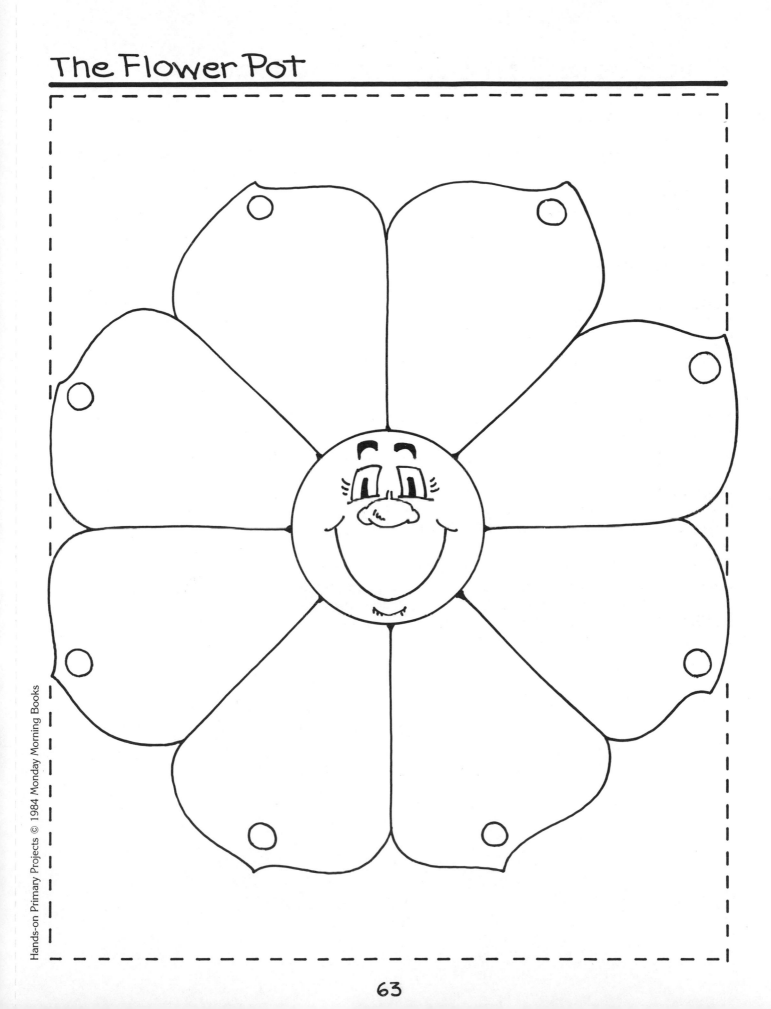

Chick and Egg Concentration

Students must match numerals and dots in this memory game.

SKILL: Associating numerals and quantities

MATERIALS:
Construction paper (green, yellow)
Heavy white paper
Clasp envelope or zip lock bag
Peel-off dots (optional)

CONSTRUCTION:
1. Trace and cut ovals out of green construction paper (at least 20).
2. Trace and cut chicks out of yellow construction paper. Glue chicks to green ovals.
3. Trace and cut eggs out of white paper.
4. Print a numeral on each chick in red marker. Put a corresponding number of dots on each egg.
5. Store chicks and eggs in clasp envelope or zip lock bag.

PROCEDURE:
1. One or several students may play this game.
2. Have student(s) turn all of the chicks and all of the eggs face down in rows.
3. Student turns over one chick and one egg at a time. If the numeral on the chick matches the number of dots on the egg, student gets to keep the pair. If not, cards are turned face down again and play continues. Winner has the most pairs.

Chick and Egg Concentration

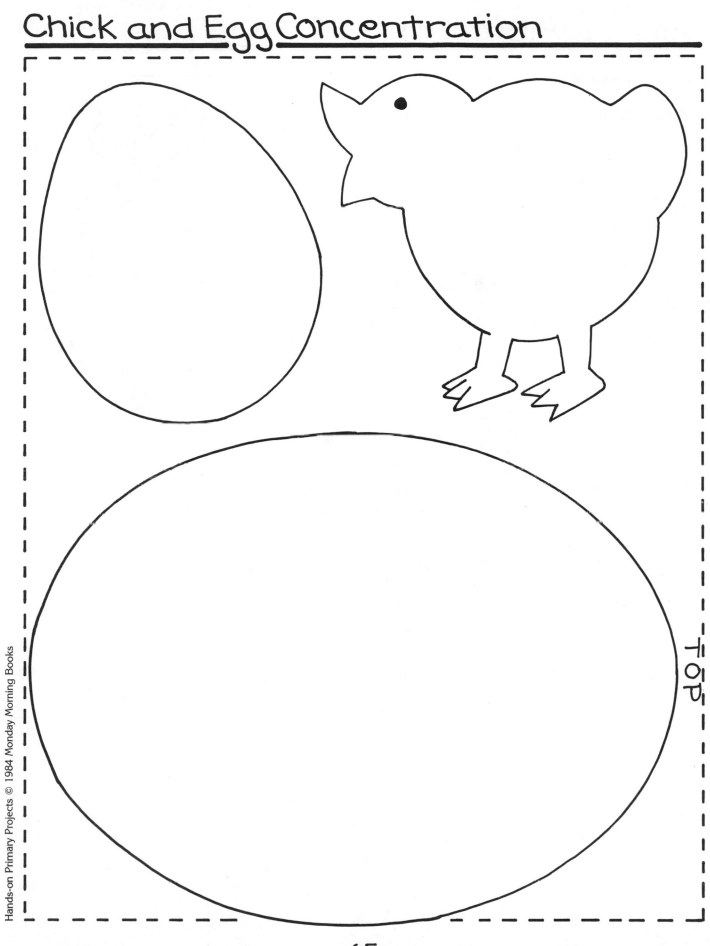

TOP

Bunny's Alphabet

Students match upper and lower case letters.

SKILL: Matching

MATERIALS:
Construction paper (12" x 17", green, pink, purple, blue)
White paper
Glue
Small manila envelope

CONSTRUCTION:
1. Color and cut out the large bunny. Glue it in the lower right corner of the green construction paper.
2. Cut 26 eggs from pink, purple, and blue construction paper. Write a lower case letter on each egg and glue in order on the green construction paper.
3. Cut 26 eggs from white paper. Write an upper case letter on each.
4. Color, cut out, and glue the small bunny on the front of the envelope. Print "Bunny's Alphabet" and store white eggs here.

PROCEDURE:
1. This activity is for one student working alone.
2. Student matches white eggs to correct colored eggs.

EXTENSION:
● Make this activity for other matches such as dots and numerals, pictures and beginning or ending sounds, pictures and vowel sounds, opposites, what's next pictures.

Bunny's Alphabet

Wake Up! It's Spring Bulletin Board

Large bunnies highlight an activities area.

MATERIALS:
Oaktag or white poster board 22" x 24"
Pink construction paper
Telephone wire

CONSTRUCTION:
1. Enlarge the patterns of the bunnies on page 59 using an opaque projector or a transparency and an overhead projector. Trace them onto oaktag or white poster board.
2. Make the bunnies' features with pink construction paper.
3. Add whiskers with telephone wire.
4. To make the bunnies stand up, first brace the poster board with a strip of cardboard glued to the back. Then cut slits between the bunnies' legs. Place additional strips of cardboard through the slits perpendicular to the brace.

Wake Up! It's Spring Board Game

This file folder game reinforces students' skills.

SKILL: Recognizing number words

MATERIALS:
File folder (preferably green)
20 game cards cut from card stock or index cards 2 1/2" x 3"
Library pocket
Peel-off dots (optional)

CONSTRUCTION:
1. Color, cut out, and glue the bunny pattern on the front of the file folder.
2. Print "Wake Up! It's Spring" in large letters on the front of the file folder.
3. Color, cut out, and glue game track inside file folder.
4. Print number words 1 – 10 in random order in the squares. (Use higher number words for older students.)
5. Put dots 1 – 10 and numerals 1 – 10 on the game cards.
6. Glue library pocket on the back of the file folder to store game cards.

PROCEDURE:
1. Two to four students may play. Each needs a game pawn.
2. Students take turns drawing a card and saying the number it represents. A correct answer enables student to move to the nearest corresponding number word on the gameboard.
3. Winner reaches the tree at the end first.

Wake Up! It's Spring Gameboard

START

Wake Up! It's Spring Gameboard

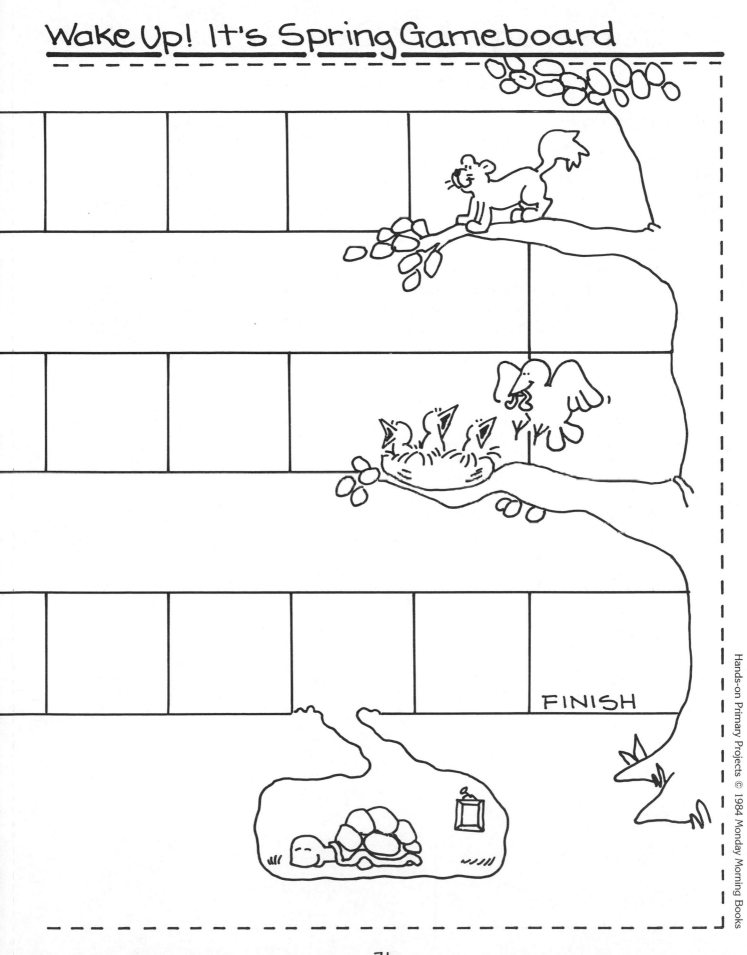

FINISH

Texture Eggs Art Center

Children rub crayons on paper over different textures.

SKILL: Naming textures

MATERIALS:
Large egg shapes cut from white paper
Peeled crayons
Variety of textured objects

CONSTRUCTION:
1. Cut enough eggs for each child to do several rubbings.
2. Set out materials for use in a special art center. You may wish to try textures such as window screening, flocked wallpaper, scrub brush, aluminum foil, needlepoint canvas, leather, carpeting, and tree leaves.

PROCEDURE:
1. Gather students around you and discuss what texture is. Let them feel and describe several of the textures in the art center.
2. Demonstrate rubbing technique. Select a texture, place a paper egg over it, and rub with the side of a crayon. Show students the results and have them describe the markings they see on the paper.
3. Encourage students to do several texture rubbings apiece.

EXTENSION:
• Challenge students to sort finished rubbings into rough and smooth, pattern and non-pattern, soft and hard textures.

Chapter Five: Safety Kid

Picture Sorting

Students sort pictures according to safety criteria.

SKILL: Classifying objects

MATERIALS:
Pocket folder
20 cards cut from card stock 5" x 8"
10 pictures (cut from magazines) of foods which are safe to eat
10 pictures (cut from magazines) of unsafe substances

CONSTRUCTION:
1. Color, cut out, and glue Safety Kid to front of folder.
2. Color Happy Face yellow and Mr. Yuk face green. Cut out and glue one face above each pocket.
3. Print these directions on the front of the folder:
        SAFETY KID — PICTURE SORTING
Find all the things that are good for you and put them in the pocket below the Happy Face. Put the things that you should never eat in the pocket below Mr. Yuk's face.

PROCEDURE:
1. One or two students can work with these cards at a time.
2. Students name each picture and tell if it is safe.

EXTENSIONS:
● Add magazines, scissors, glue, and blank cards to a work station so that students can make additional sorting cards.
● Brainstorm a list of products whose label should carry the Mr. Yuk symbol. Duplicate the list and send it home with students.

Picture Sorting

Picture Sorting

Hands-on Primary Projects © 1984 Monday Morning Books

Signal Cards

Students use symbols to indicate safe and unsafe things.

SKILL: Identifying safe and unsafe objects

MATERIALS:
6" cardboard circles (enough for entire class)

CONSTRUCTION:
1. Trace or duplicate a Happy Face and a Mr. Yuk pattern for each student.
2. Color each Happy Face yellow and each Mr. Yuk green.
3. Glue a Happy Face to one side of each circle and a Mr. Yuk face to the other side.

PROCEDURE:
1. Distribute signal cards to students.
2. Display cards from picture sorting activity, one at a time. Students should hold up the appropriate side of their picture cards to show they understand which things are safe and which are unsafe.

EXTENSIONS:
● Punch a hole at the top of each signal card and thread yarn through it. Tie a knot and allow students to wear signal cards around the neck. (Note: For some students this may be an easier way to use signal cards; for others it may not.)
● You may wish to introduce the concept of safe and unsafe objects by starting with the signal cards.

Safety Kid Bulletin Board

Students see empty containers of dangerous materials.

SKILL: Recognizing containers of harmful substances

MATERIALS:
Oaktag
Yarn
Clean, empty containers for harmful substances

CONSTRUCTION:
1. Enlarge the pattern on page 73 using an opaque projector or a transparency which you make and an overhead projector.
2. Trace the pattern onto oaktag. Cut out and color it.
3. Make hair with 5" lengths of heavy yarn. Glue yarn to Safety Kid, then fray out the ends. If you plan to laminate the figure, do so before gluing on the hair.
4. Hang up Safety Kid and the empty containers with pins or thumbtacks. You may wish to use containers from bleach, dishwashing soap, toilet bowl cleaner, cough medicine, aspirin, and prescription drugs as examples.

PROCEDURE:
1. Gather students around the bulletin board and introduce Safety Kid, whose job it is to show children which things they should never play with or put in their mouths.
2. Call on students to identify the substances which come in containers displayed on the bulletin board. Explain why these things are dangerous.
3. Teach students what they should do in case of accidental poisoning. (Tell an adult immediately; show the adult the container of the substance; call 911 or other local emergency telephone number for medical help.)

Stay Away From Mr. Yuk Game

This game reinforces the recognition of safety symbols.

SKILL: Discriminating between symbols

MATERIALS:
Oaktag or poster board cut 12" x 18"
Construction paper
Small blank cards
Zip lock bag
One die

CONSTRUCTION:
1. Color Safety Kid and Mr. Yuk.
2. Glue gameboard to oaktag or poster board.
3. Color Happy Faces yellow and Mr. Yuk faces green. Cut out and glue at intervals along the game track. One Mr. Yuk means move back one space, two Happy Faces mean move forward 2 spaces, and so on. Use as many as three faces on one game track.
4. Write questions or problems on game cards. Examples: math flash cards, money value cards, sight words, shapes, colors, upper and lower case letters. Store cards in zip lock bag.

PROCEDURE:
1. Two to four students may play.
2. Each player in turn rolls a die and moves that number of spaces on the game track. If the player lands on a Happy Face, he or she may move forward an additional space. If the player lands on a Mr. Yuk face, he or she must move back one space. If the player lands on a blank space, he or she must draw a game card and answer a question or problem.
3. Winner is the first student to arrive at Finish.

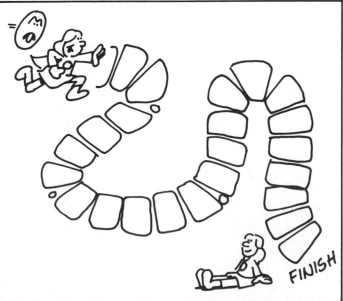

Stay Away from Mr. Yuk Game

Stay Away from Mr. Yuk Game

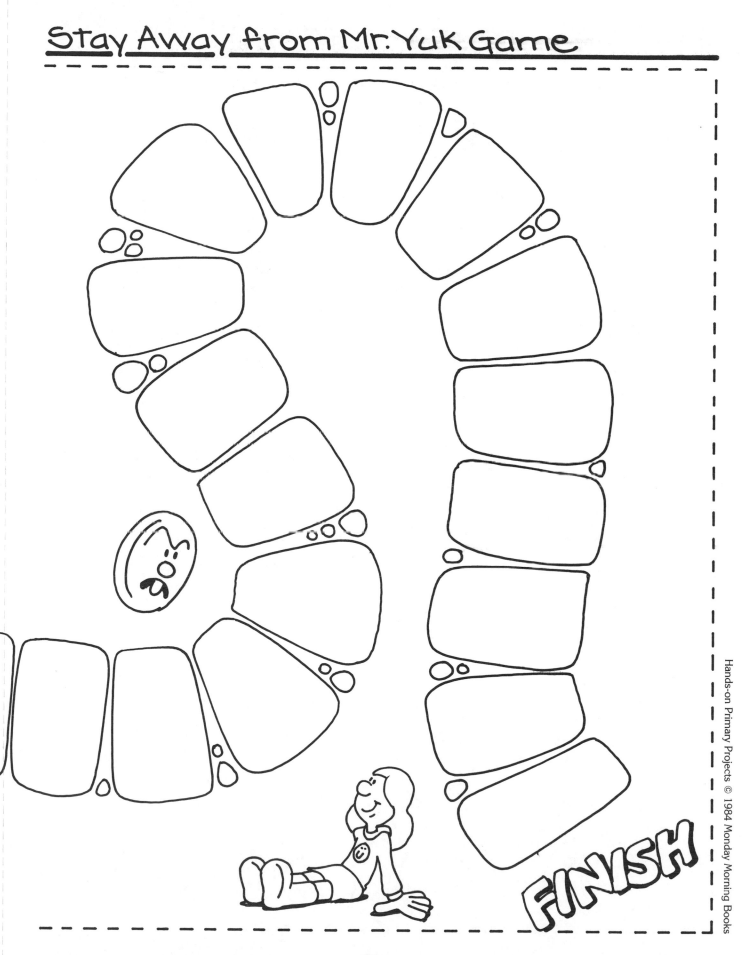

FINISH

Hands-on Primary Projects © 1984 Monday Morning Books

Stay Away from Mr. Yuk Game

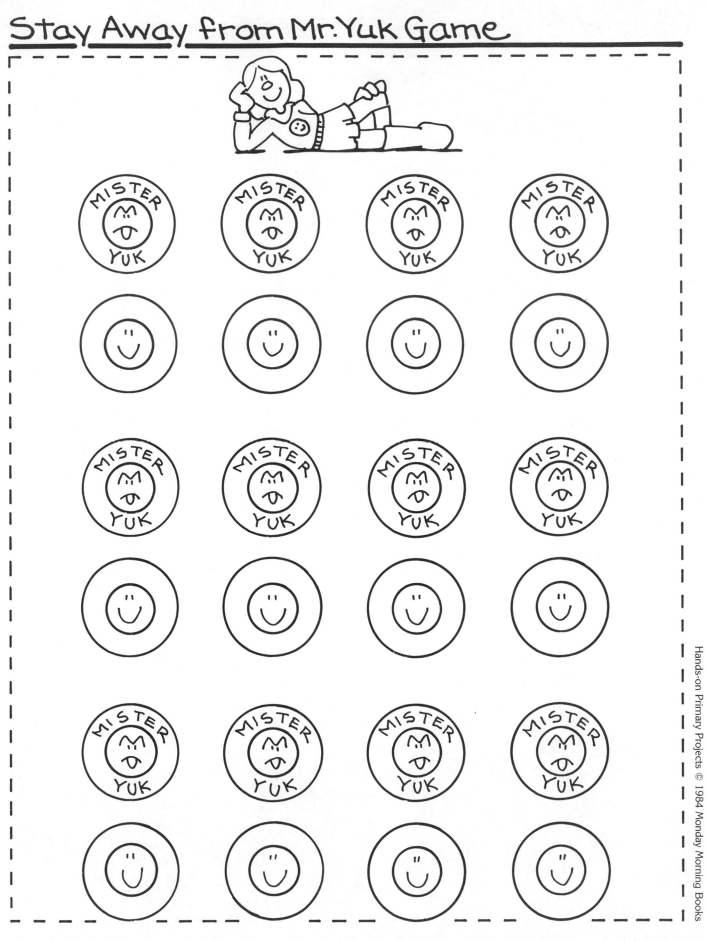

Chapter Six: Neanderthal Ned and the Dinosaur

Vanishing Act

Students arrange bones in size order to make them vanish.

SKILL: Sequencing

MATERIALS:
File folder
Six strips of black construction paper 8 1/2" x 4"
Zip lock bag

CONSTRUCTION:
1. Color, cut out, and glue Ned, the dinosaur, and the large bone on the front of the file folder.
2. Print "Vanishing Act" on the bone and these directions on the file folder: "Dinosaurs vanished long, long ago. Neanderthal Ned will never find a living dinosaur. Pretend you can make Ned's dinosaur bones disappear."
3. Cut out the bones and the "?" Glue one on each strip.
4. Staple zip lock bag inside folder to store bones.

PROCEDURE:
1. This activity is for one student.
2. Ask the student to arrange the bones in order from largest to smallest.

EXTENSIONS:
● Write a six-line story about Ned and the dinosaur, one sentence on the back of each strip. Students can sequence the bones first, or the story, then turn the strips over.
● Have older students write their own six-sentence stories on strips of paper for classmates to sequence.

Vanishing Act

Vanishing Act

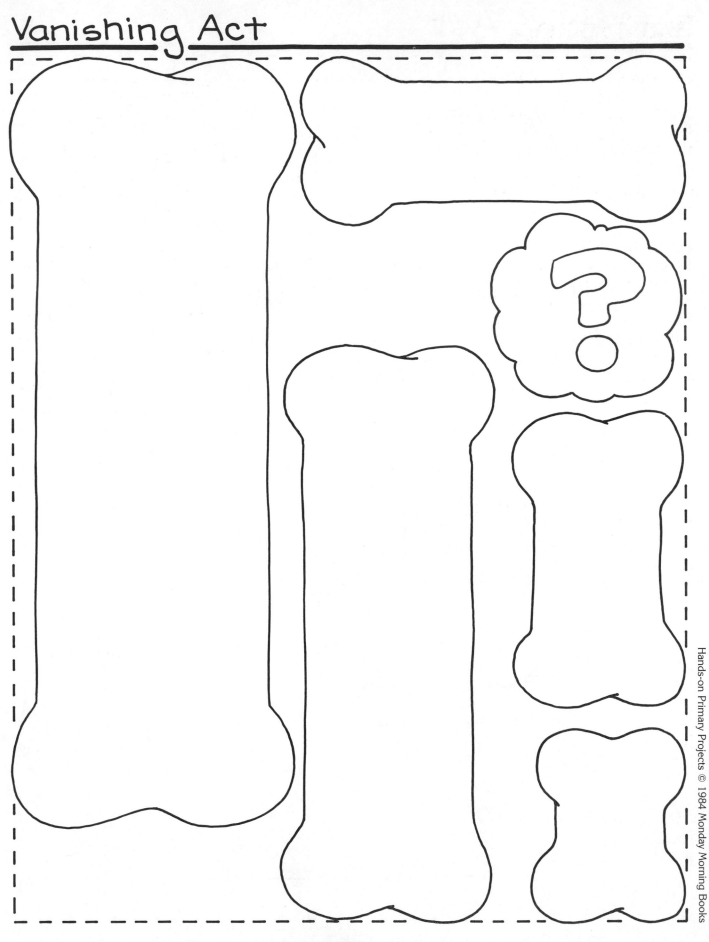

Hands-on Primary Projects © 1984 Monday Morning Books

Big Bones

Students measure and record the length of dinosaur bones.

SKILL: Linear measurement

MATERIALS:
File folder
Heavy beige construction paper
Zip lock bag

CONSTRUCTION:
1. Color, cut out, and glue the pictures of Ned and the large bone on the front of the file folder.
2. Cut out the ruler and worksheet. Glue them to the left side of the open folder.
3. Trace the bone patterns on beige construction paper. Cut out and laminate or cover with clear contact paper.
4. Staple a zip lock bag inside the folder on the right to store the bones.

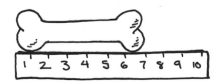

PROCEDURE:
1. This activity is for one or two students.
2. Show students how to measure each bone and write down its length. Be sure they put the end of the bone to the end of the ruler.

EXTENSIONS:
• Make this a self-checking activity by adding an answer key to the back of the file folder.
• Use this activity to teach estimating and verifying.

Big Bones

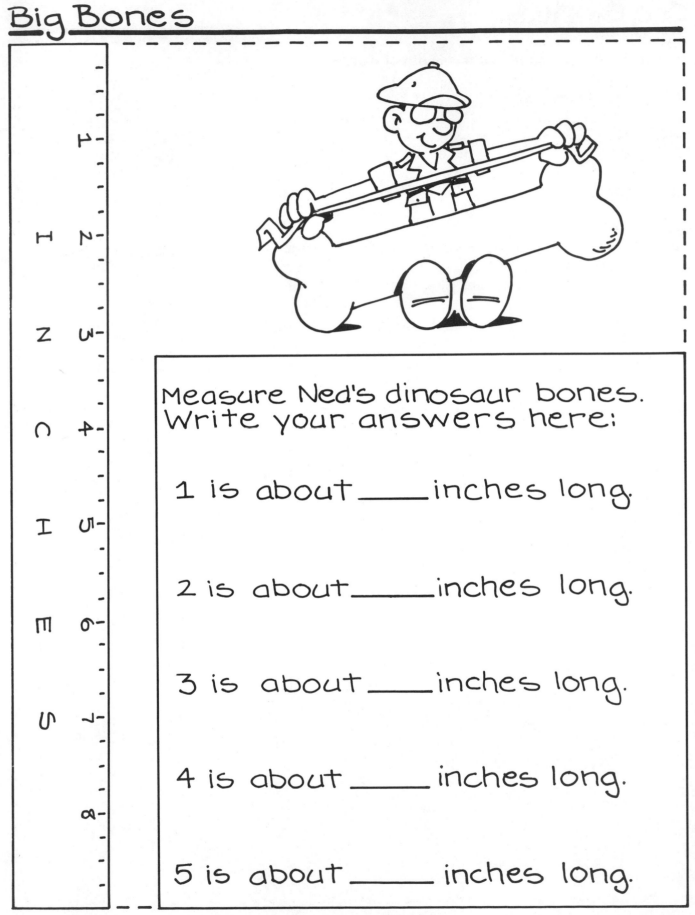

INCHES

1 2 3 4 5 6 7 8

Measure Ned's dinosaur bones.
Write your answers here:

1 is about ____ inches long.

2 is about ____ inches long.

3 is about ____ inches long.

4 is about ____ inches long.

5 is about ____ inches long.

Hands-on Primary Projects © 1984 Monday Morning Books

Big Bones

Scrambled Dinosaur Eggs

Students complete sentences with words built on "og."

SKILLS: Recognizing "og" words, deducing words from context

MATERIALS:
File folder
Heavy white paper
Zip lock bag

CONSTRUCTION:
1. Color, cut out, and glue Ned and the dinosaur to front of folder. Cut out a large egg shape, print "Scrambled Dinosaur Eggs" on it, and glue it to front of folder.

2. Color and cut out picture of Og, list of scrambled answers, and answer sheet. Glue these inside folder on left. Write these directions: "Help Caveman Og unscramble these dinosaur eggs." Laminate or cover with clear plastic.
3. Cut 10 eggs from white paper. Copy these sentences:
    (1.) I like to teach my pet _____ tricks.
    (2.) In the farmer's pen were six _____.
    (3.) Sometimes when I run I like to _____.
    (4.) After a rain, the ground gets _____.
    (5.) Cranberries grow in a _____.
    (6.) Divers wear _____ to see under
        water.
    (7.) It's hard to see in this thick _____.
    (8.) In December we drink egg _____.
    (9.) The snake crawled under the _____.
   (10.) Another name for a tadpole is a
        poly_____.
4. Staple zip lock bag inside folder on right to store eggs.
5. Glue the answer sheet on the back of the folder.

PROCEDURE:
1. This activity is for one student working alone.
2. Student writes numbered answers, checks them on back.

Scrambled Dinosaur Eggs

Scrambled Answers

bog   hogs

wog   jog

dog   log

fog   nog

goggles   soggy

WRITE YOUR ANSWERS HERE

1 _____   6 _____

2 _____   7 _____

3 _____   8 _____

4 _____   9 _____

5 _____   10 _____

CHECK YOUR ANSWERS ON BACK OF FOLDER

Scrambled Dinosaur Eggs

ANSWERS

1 dog	6 goggles
2 hogs	7 fog
3 jog	8 nog
4 soggy	9 log
5 bog	10 wog

Hands-on Primary Projects © 1984 Monday Morning Books

Neanderthal Ned's Board Game

This game can be used to reinforce a variety of skills.

SKILL: To be decided by the teacher

MATERIALS:
Poster board (brown or green)
White paper

CONSTRUCTION:
1. Color and cut out Ned, the cave, and the dinosaur. Glue them to the poster board.
2. Cut 20 small bones from white paper and glue them to the poster board to form the game track.
3. Add extra moves with the footprints:

     caveman footprints = go ahead two bones
     dinosaur footprints = go ahead three bones
     fossils = go ahead one bone

4. On the large bone print: "Neanderthal Ned, the noted paleontologist, is looking for an ancient dinosaur cave. Help Ned get to the cave. Do you think Ned will be surprised?"
5. Laminate gameboard and add skills with an erasable transparency pen. In this way you can change the skills as your students progress. Examples: number or letter recognition.

PROCEDURE:
1. This game is for two to four students.
2. Students throw dice or turn a spinner to determine how many bones they may advance. Students must be able to perform the skill specified on the destination bone in order to stay there.

Neanderthal Ned's Game

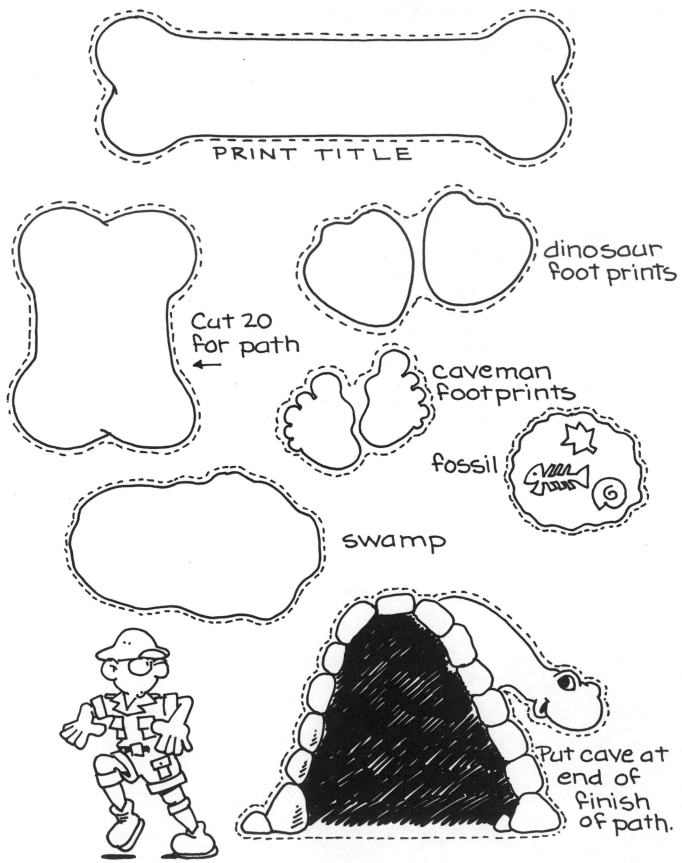

PRINT TITLE

Cut 20 for path

dinosaur foot prints

caveman footprints

fossil

swamp

Put cave at end of finish of path.

Hands-on Primary Projects © 1984 Monday Morning Books

Neanderthal Ned's Bulletin Board

Large pictures introduce students to these activities.

MATERIALS:
Oaktag or poster board
Wallpaper in various patterns

CONSTRUCTION:
1. Enlarge the patterns on page 83 by using an opaque projector or a transparency and an overhead projector.
2. Trace the designs on oaktag or poster board and cut out.
3. Make Ned's clothes and shoes from wallpaper and glue on.

PROCEDURE:
1. Hang Ned and the dinosaur on a bulletin board near the activities in this chapter.
2. Print "Neanderthal Ned" and "Dinosaur" on two index cards. Gather your students in front of bulletin board and introduce characters as you staple name cards beside them.
3. Discuss dinosaurs with students, giving them information about age, size, diet, and habitat.

Dinosaur Art

Students create their own dinosaurs in an art center.

SKILL: Drawing, pasting

MATERIALS:
Art paper
Strips of brown and green construction paper
Crayons
Scissors
Paste

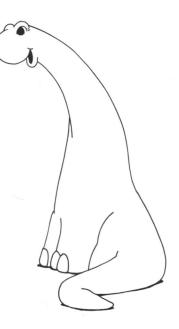

CONSTRUCTION:
1. Put large art paper, crayons, scissors, paste, and strips of brown and green construction paper in your art center.
2. Over the art center hang a sign which says: "Dinosaur Art — We know that dinosaurs were reptiles. They had scales on their bodies. Draw a big dinosaur. Cut out paper scales and glue them on your dinosaur."

PROCEDURE:
1. Demonstrate this activity for students by drawing a dinosaur. Use the pattern as a sample, if necessary. Color your dinosaur, then cut and paste on paper scales.
2. Provide a space for students to display their work when they have finished.

EXTENSION:
● Explain to students why dinosaurs had scales and how scales helped dinosaurs to live.

Chapter Seven: Dana's Department Store

How To Make Dana's Department Store

This stand-up chart is the setting for all the sorting and categorizing activities in this chapter.

MATERIALS:

Poster board 23" x 28"
1 library pocket
4 colored peel-off dots
Sturdy paper strip 2" x 22"

CONSTRUCTION:

1. Cut 9 inches off the length of the poster board. Tape the shorter piece back to the longer piece to make the front flap of the chart.
2. Cut out and glue the windows to the outside of the flap.
3. Open the flap and glue the 8 store departments inside.
4. Color, cut out, and glue on the name "Dana's" and the picture of the elevator operator, Mr. Mac.
5. Make the library pocket into a freight elevator to carry sorting cards to the right floor. Cut out a rectangle 2" x 2 1/2" from the top of the front portion. Cut 2 horizontal slits 2 1/2" long in the back portion to let the paper strip fit through like a belt. Cut a hole 3/4" in diameter at the top of the library pocket.
6. Slide elevator onto paper strip and fasten ends of strip to chart. Apply peel-off dots to the strip in line with each floor. Number each dot, starting with 1 at the bottom.

Library pocket

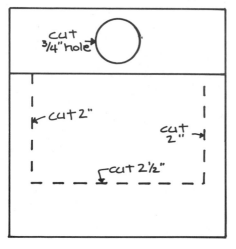

Front of Department Store

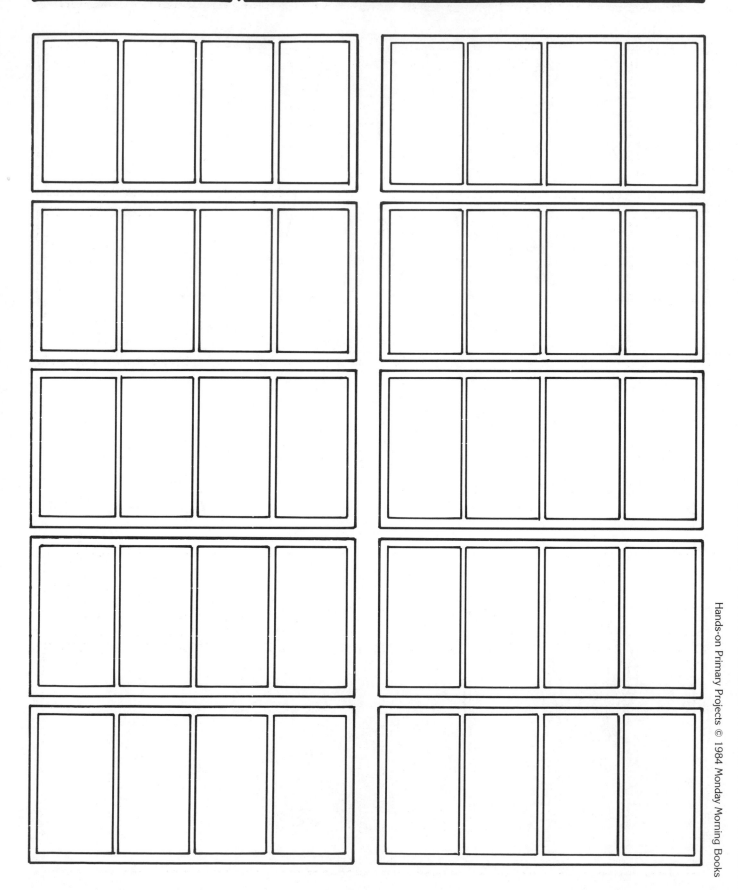

Front of Department Store

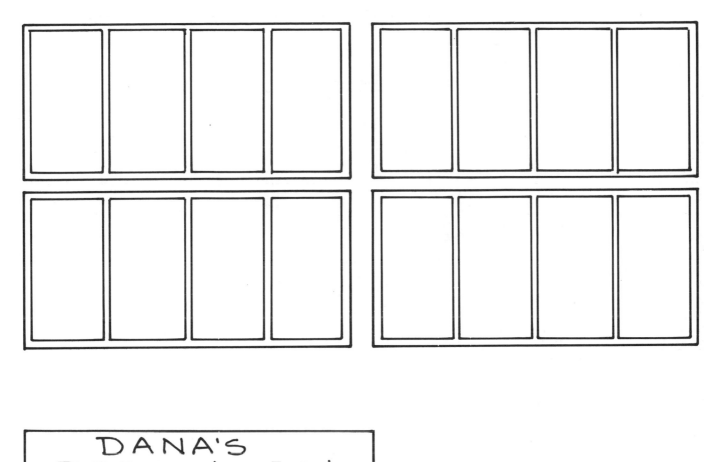

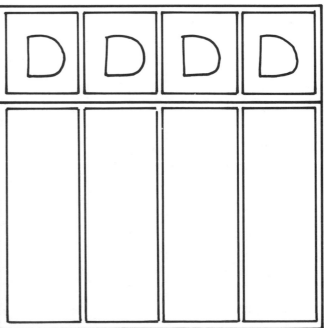

DANA'S
Department
Store

Store Departments

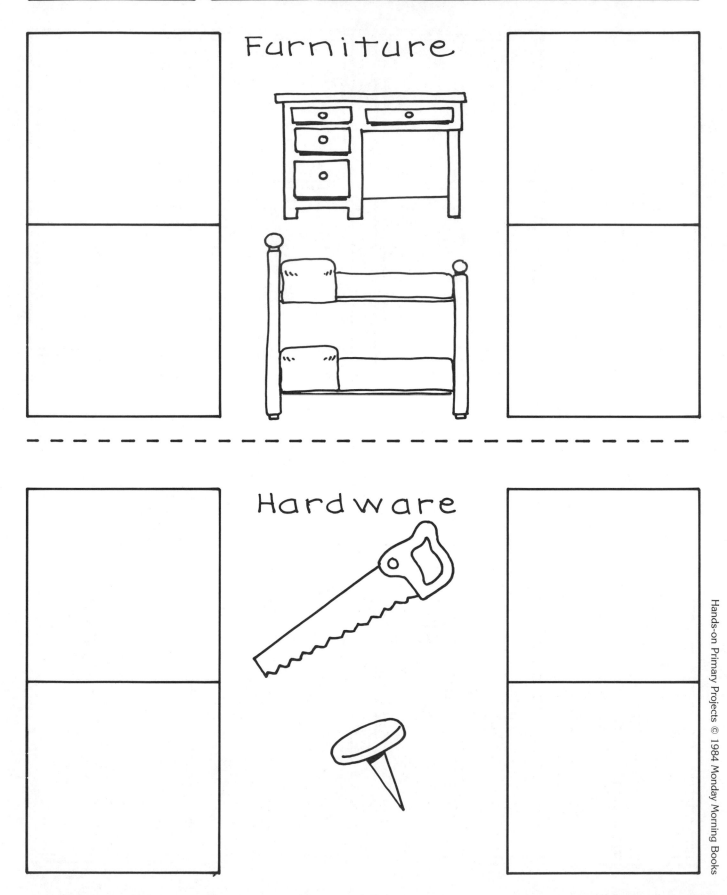

Furniture

Hardware

Hands-on Primary Projects © 1984 Monday Morning Books

Store Departments

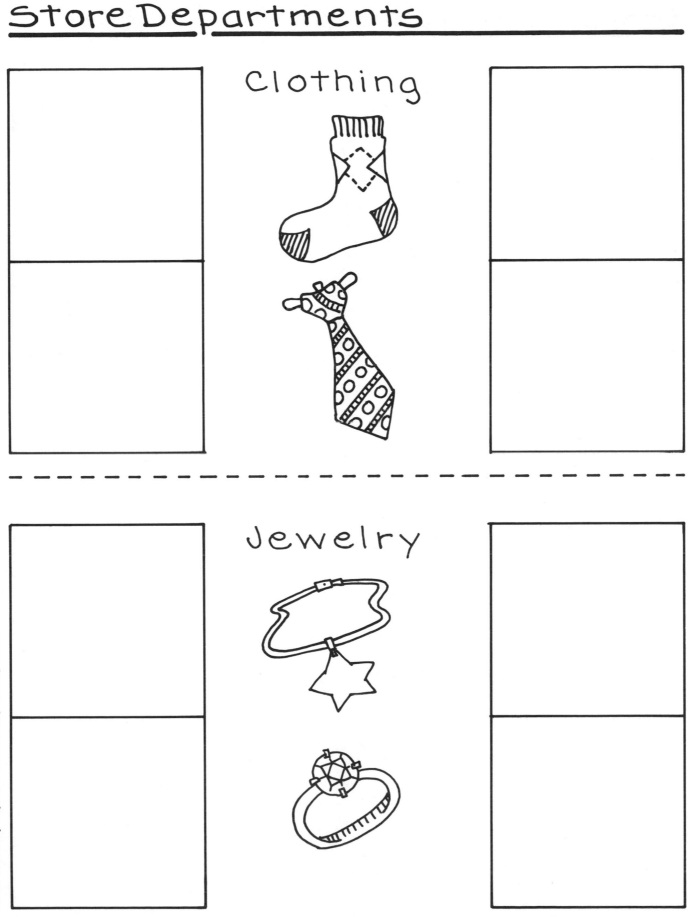

Clothing

Jewelry

Store Departments

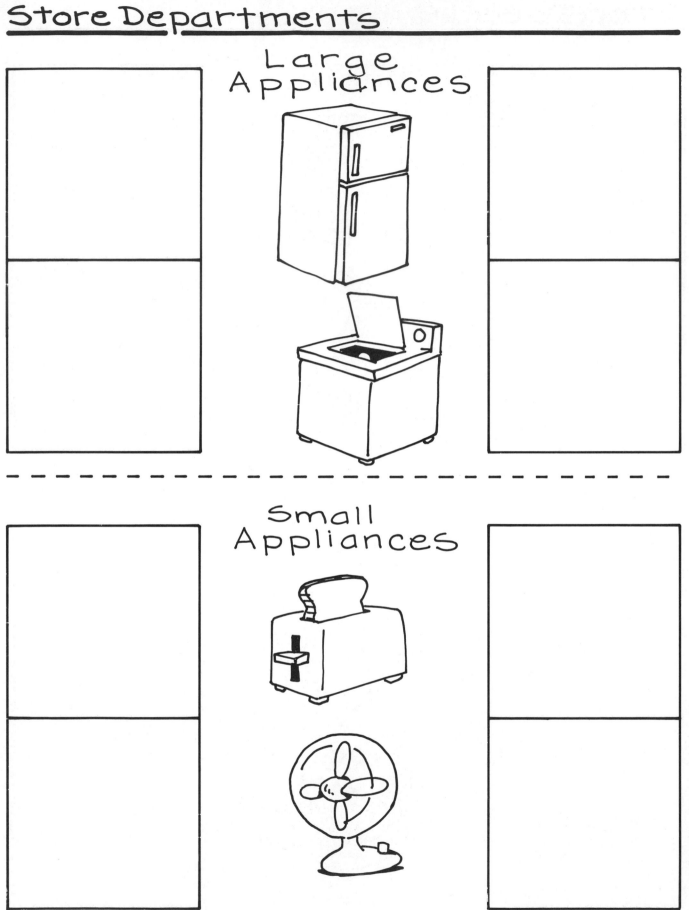

Large Appliances

Small Appliances

Store Departments

TOYS

Shoes

Store Sorting Cards

Students deliver items to correct departments in the store.

SKILL: Categorizing

MATERIALS:
48 cards cut from heavy paper 2 1/2" x 2 1/2"
Zip lock bag
Pocket folder
Rubber cement

CONSTRUCTION:
1. Color, cut out, and glue 48 pictures to heavy cards.
2. Laminate the store and all the cards. Put a generous amount of rubber cement on the back of each card and allow it to air dry. This process will enable the cards to stick to the store.
3. Store the cards in a zip lock bag.
4. Color, cut out, and glue the pattern of the door and the word "Dana's" on the front of the pocket folder. Store sorting cards and money cards in this folder.

PROCEDURE:
1. Tell students they are going to work in Dana's Department Store. They must take each item sold in the store up on the elevator and deliver it to its proper department.
2. Demonstrate the elevator. Also show students how to make sorting cards stick in the proper place.
3. Encourage students to check each other's work.

EXTENSION:
● Duplicate store departments and sorting cards as worksheets. Students cut apart cards and paste them in appropriate departments.

Store Sorting Cards

Toys and Shoes

Kite	Sneaker	Slippers	Boot
High Heel Pump	Jack in a Box	Bike	Game

Clothing and Jewelry

Dress	Necklace	Blouse	Wrist watch
Ring	Bracelet	Shirt	Sweater

Store Sorting Cards

Furniture and Hardware

Hammer	Screwdriver	Table	Sofa
Hose	Nail	Dresser	Chair

Small and Large Appliances

Clock	Stove	Lamp	Vacuum Sweeper
Refrigerator	Toaster	Telephone	Washer

Hands-on Primary Projects © 1984 Monday Morning Books

Money Cards

Students match price tags with correct coins.

SKILL: Recognizing coin values

MATERIALS:
32 cards cut from heavy paper 2 1/2" x 2 1/2"
Two zip lock bags
Rubber cement

CONSTRUCTION:
1. Color, cut out, and glue pictures onto heavy cards.
2. Laminate the cards and apply rubber cement to the back of each. Allow to air dry for stickiness.
3. Store the cards in the zip lock bags. The bags may be kept in the pocket folder used for the sorting cards.

PROCEDURE:
1. This game is for two or more players.
2. Players turn all price tag cards face down in a pile and place all coin cards face up in rows in front of the store.
3. Each student draws a price tag card and takes it up the elevator to the proper department. The next student finds the correct coin card for that item. If the coin card is correct, that player may draw an item card.
4. Students continue taking turns finding correct coin cards until all item cards have been played. Winner is the student with the most correct answers.

EXTENSION:
• Use item and money cards for a game of Concentration. Students must match price tag cards with correct coin cards to make pairs. Winner has the most pairs.

Money Cards

20¢ Slippers	5¢ Pen	5¢ Shoe	25¢ Ring
50¢ Watch	50¢ Boot	25¢ Necklace	15¢ Sneaker
20¢ Jack in a Box	6¢ Telephone	10¢ Clock	50¢ Vacuum
25¢ Lamp	6¢ Kite	15¢ Game	25¢ Bike

Money Cards

Store Bulletin Board

A large paper figure introduces these activities.

MATERIALS:
Oaktag or poster board
Three buttons
Telephone wire

CONSTRUCTION:
1. Enlarge the pattern using an opaque projector or a transparency and an overhead projector.
2. Trace the pattern onto the oaktag. Color or use construction paper to make his clothes, shoes, and hat.
3. Laminate, if desired, then glue on buttons and glasses made of telephone wire.
4. Display Mr. Mac on a bulletin board with letters that say:
   WHAT IS MR. MAC'S JOB?

PROCEDURE:
1. Use the title of the bulletin board to start a group discussion.
2. Record student answers on sentence strips and staple around Mr. Mac.
3. Be sure to clarify all of the jobs students mention. Examples:
   Salesperson - takes people's money
   Elevator operator - runs the elevator
   Manager - sees that the clerks do their job
   Security person - keeps the store safe
   Stock room person - brings in deliveries
   Buyer - chooses items to be sold